How to Be a Successful Artist:
Drawing Yourself Out of Depression
Katy Fryd

New Edition

Published by Three Sock Press, U.K.

ISBN: 978-0-9935477-0-6

In memory of Gordon and Caroline,
two of the best teachers, gone far too soon,
their legacy will live on through the many pupils
they have inspired

"Take the squeegee at a forty-five degree angle and push." - G.R.

Foreword

Katy's experience of depression is detailed so eloquently, both in words and pictures. She injects much humour and honesty into her journey with an illness which is still greatly misunderstood and stigmatised in today's society. A must read for anyone that's ever lived with depression, and also for those who want to gain an insight into the mind of someone suffering from it.

- Jonny Benjamin

Preface

When I was a child, after we had satiated our appetites (or not quite satiated our appetites as the case usually was) my mother used to produce a quiz, IQ test or a can you spot the grammatical error in this text from a newspaper, magazine, book or poster that she had read that day. We used to sit working out the answer for fun or perhaps for the love and attention of our parents. (She still does this to this day.)

I thought about getting an editor for this book, I know I should. English, or at least English how it is supposed to be written is not one of my strengths. However, I decided, to please me or to please yourself you may go through this book circling my errors with a big red pen. I think that would be more fun and a lot cheaper for me than paying an editor. And you are welcome to inform me of mistakes for future editions.

I also have some difficulty with syntax. But I think that is okay, it just means you are hearing my authentic voice through your reading.

The following collection of drawings were exhibited in a group exhibition paid for by the charity MIND, called M.A.D. Art (making a difference) held at the Truman Brewery, Brick Lane, London in 2007. I will always be grateful to them for the opportunity to exhibit in London as it really ignited my passion to take my art seriously again, which was such a big and essential part of my identity before becoming a mother. And I hope to repay them and other charities that I am interested in, throughout the course of my career.

This book started out it's life as a book about recovery from depression, but when I read it again now, it screams post traumatic stress disorder too. So if you do find yourself relating to a lot of the images you may want to investigate further into that subject.

I would also like to say thank you to the people who helped in the production of this book with their friendship and support of my vision in the very early stages and have been waiting for their copies for far too long. A massive thank you to Liz Garnett, Susan Smith, Susan Jane Sims, Onno, Jess Dyson, Diane Fryd, Lucy Wildblood and Lizzie Whittingham and all my other friends who keep me positive. Thank you also to Andy Lutey, as our discussions together may have influenced some of my opinions on the topics in this book. A thank you must also go to Jonny Benjamin for being so kind in replying to my request, taking the time to read my book and writing a foreword for me.

- Katy Fryd, September 2013

Introduction

It makes me sad to know that a great many talented artists end up not fulfilling their dreams, when other less gifted beings are thrown into the limelight. It frustrates me that some of these people go through such dark, internal struggles and that the beauty and inspiration which they could create will never see the light of day. This book is for those people. I often wish I could persuade these creative individuals to be the best they could be, to get past their own negative internal monologue and just begin.

So this is a bit of my story, of a time in my life when I survived through a period of darkness, a time where I lost hope for the future. I want to ignite that lost spark of hope in others. I want to show that, in the future, the world will be more colourful for them. And I want to encourage them to draw themselves out of depression.

Prologue

As far as I can make out, there is good and bad art and both are either hidden from view or paraded in front of the masses or somewhere in between.

If a fantastic piece of work remains largely unknown about, it is almost as though it didn't exist. Like the tree felled in the forest that no one hears, all the meaning or beauty of an unseen work of art is wasted. Worse still, are the many works of art that are left uncreated, remaining just a twinkle in the artist's eye in this world, sparking many a parallel universe.

And artwork is so very subjective. I am lucky to have more confidence now, having sold work and had some great compliments from people I respect, so that I know it is not my work that is the problem preventing me from fame and fortune. It's much more likely to be a marketing issue.

Artists need to reach the masses just to find a small number of supportive patrons and I would argue that the old fashioned way of using galleries and exhibitions is changing. The Internet is bound to have an effect on this, as it has on other industries. Although, to their relief, I'm sure we will still need the galleries for the grand spectacle and to touch, feel and soak in the art in the flesh.

Marketing and business are dirty words to the pure artist but words that we must take seriously if we are going to have any effect and longevity. Up until recently I thought I could survive living as minimally as possible and not have to create anything I didn't want to. I still think it is possible to only create what we want to, as artists, but we need a strategy to do that and still manage to have food to eat.

My style of art is not for everybody and if it were, I don't think it would be very good work. My aim is to create work that is not decorative or for putting above sofas, unless you are a more discerning art lover. My work is trying to say a lot more than just being attractive to look at.

That's where I realise I am probably not a pure painter at heart. There are many artists honing their craft to make beautiful, attractive work where the purpose is to sell and make money. I think painting is purely one of the many mediums that I use to help convey feelings, my understanding of the world, my take on aspects of psychology and the humour or pain of life.

There is also the element of 'The Emperor's new clothes' about art. People who are not quite sure about their tastes need someone else to tell them something is good before they are willing to invest.

I am at a stage now, where I need an income from my art to survive and I can see why many go down the pretty domestic 'sofa' art route but each time I think this would be a good idea, there seems to be an invisible force stopping me. I just cannot bring myself to go there.

When I was at school I used to do a lot of work on still lifes. My art teacher would set these up and we would work on them. The end results were pretty interesting and beautiful pieces.

Sometimes, I think I should try to go back to these. But it disheartens me that I may put in a huge effort and have just as much trouble selling these, amongst the amount of similar work available. They would also take a huge amount of time to create. Time is something I feel I have very little of and therefore need to spend what little I do have effectively. My time is restricted by family life and the constant and possibly irrational fear of sudden and unexpected death.

I am clearly not interested in making pretty work for beauty's sake, I want to make work that means something much more and that might even change the world for the better! Though, if you are someone who takes delight in creating beautiful work then that is great for you! And sometimes, and maybe this is the key, work can have a lot of meaning and also be beautiful and aesthetic, so perhaps that is something to strive for.

When worrying about the type of art we make I think we have to remember the number one rule of art - that there ain't no rules. If you play the game by other people's rules, it is going to be tough. So - Make your own rules! If it goes against the grain you will just be starting a new movement or genre.

After a few years of having the attitude of "You've got to be in it to win it!" and entering many prestigious art awards and competitions and not getting very far, I found it disheartening and costly. I truly believe there is little point entering, unless you are well known on the London art scene or have been exhibiting in London or other major cities within the last year, or are known in certain social circles. And these competitions can go on and on about how they are 'Open' and that there is the possibility that anyone can get through, but I truly believe those chances are minuscule and not worth the cost. After all, what will entry get you anyway? Prestige? Kudos? Yes, but there are other ways to get this. Here's an idea - work on art projects that could potentially make national news for more than a day and be more focussed on you as an individual artist, rather than you as one of a group of people, despite the fact you have managed to get through a subjective selection process to exhibit in a major exhibition.

Another tip and one of the best pieces of advice I ever received from my tutors in Hull was to "document, document, document!" I suppose the emphasis was especially important due to many of us doing performance work.

I have every intention of becoming a great artist during my lifetime, one to reckon with Picasso or Hockney. Why not? So I think now is as good a time as any to start documenting my old and current work. This is why I am writing these books, registering them with a major bibliographic database and sending them to the five British libraries in the UK to be stored for eternity.

I would recommend this to up and coming artists. It takes a lot of guts to hold yourself in high enough esteem to write your thoughts down and suggest they may be valuable to other people and artists. But I try to think of it like this, how many times have you read an autobiography and thought it really resonated with you, made you feel happier and strengthened your values on life? Like the internal pat on the back when you cleverly guess a murderer correctly in a detective television program. You were right all along.

So I have started with this book which documents the drawings I made at a pivotal point in my life. A point where I realized that I needed to be a creator, I needed to have art in my life to survive. Purely being a mother or a wife was not enough. At this stage I was so depressed about the world I could not bring myself to work in colour, but managed to produce some ink drawings. I think these drawings are important to help understand depression in visual terms.

'Drawing yourself out of depression' is a catalogue of artwork containing a very black humour.

In the text I will mention "posh school" and that needs to be elucidated upon. For most of my childhood I grew up in what I would call financial poverty, though my parents did very well providing for us. We had little money for food but I was very fortunate that my father owned a big house and large garden and fields, so we could frolic all day long and get up to mischief. A lot of food was also grown in the garden. Dishes made from the home grown food included: rhubarb crumble, gooseberry fool, and fennel soup. Oh! Whilst talking about foods, I mustn't forget to mention the junket, made every so often when the milk couldn't be drunk in time and was starting to go off. For those that haven't had the pleasure, junket is milk jelly.

Occasionally my dad would bring us a special treat of a bin bag liner full of cream cakes and sugary doughnuts, that the baker was going to throw out. My siblings and I stole misshapen peppermints from sacks in the garden. They had been heavily discounted and were meant for the bees my dad was farming. There was another occasion when we had the chest freezer full of chocolate ice cream, where the manufacturer had added double cocoa by mistake and it was therefore not fit for human consumption. We mixed it with vanilla and it was fine. We were forbidden from having too much though, which is when I figured out if I put it in a mug and compacted it, I could get away with having far more than if I put it in a bowl.

We delighted in the sack of clothes we received from the local priest, who had been given them as a donation to the poor, from fellow parishioners with slightly older children. My sister had been teased once with a rhyme that suggested our clothes came from a well known supermarket: Lets all go to [Insert name of supermarket], where [Insert name of child] buys her best clothes. If only they knew the reality was much worse. I would have loved to have bought my clothes in a supermarket.

No money was wasted on shoes until we started school. We wore flip flops, Wellington boots and bare feet. My party trick was to walk on sharp stones without flinching as my soles had become as tough as asbestos.

However, aged eleven I did get an assisted place, through a government scheme, to a private secondary school. This is where I learned my posh voice which I have since downplayed but it does come back when mixing with certain well spoken people. There are those who shalt remain nameless, who have said I should keep quiet about the fact I got my school place for free but with my more recently discovered socialist principles, I would be far more embarrassed if people thought I went there because my family could have afforded to pay for it and chose to do so. Having said that, recent events have made me realise there is a place for independent schools, especially for children with special educational needs or disabilities. And maybe, just maybe, I only survived my teenage years because I went to that school.

I think the education in private schools is excellent, save a few points. And I wouldn't know exactly what a state secondary is really like to compare it to. The only example I had was 'Grange Hill', therefore I was pretty terrified of the idea of going to my local comprehensive. From a parent's point of view, I think the state schools are focussing more and more on the wrong things. For example, the fact that it is vitally important to have a perfect uniform, allegedly to get the pupils to be smart for the workplace. More like crushing the one bit of independent spirit left in these vile places. After all, the fact that any child expecting to attend University is going to have at least three years of being a scruffy student. And surely anyone can learn tidiness, smartness and timekeeping within a very short time, if they need to. They don't need seven years of it, to drum it into them. One of the suggestions from a teacher friend, was that if they come down hard on the uniform rule, the kids will be less likely to misbehave in other ways. I doubt this very much. The more restrictions you place on someone, the more inventive they get in breaking the rules and getting away with it. Being brought up Catholic, I know that better than anyone, but that is another story, another book.

Talking of presenting oneself leads me to consider the clothing snobs. You know, the ones who can't bear a hole in anything. A slight bit of wear and tear, a hole, and the item gets thrown away. I don't feel a connection to these people and it is a false snobbery anyway. No doubt the aristocracy couldn't give a damn about holes in clothes. There is something romantic and comforting about holes in jumpers.

However, humans are a foolish race, and there is a certain power to clothes by which people judge you - even me. I'm not sure even I would believe a talk from a guy telling me how he'd made his millions if he was dressed like a homeless man. The smarter you are the more you can fool the public, or perhaps I should say make an impression. Certainly if trying to make sales using video marketing one can add more credence by dressing more successfully.

An artist can get away with a 'look', a style. In fact it helps to have one, as you become more memorable in people's minds. I'm still working on figuring out mine. As I was making the final touches to this book I accidentally burned my cornea and had to wear a baseball hat and some wraparound shades for a week. I was tempted to stick with that look. I could tell that people weren't entirely sure if I was a celebrity trying to walk around incognito or not! However half way through the week I realised I looked more like Roland Rat than anyone else.

These are the negatives and the reasons not to choose a private school education - being surrounded by girls who said things like "it's okay to drop litter as it gives the cleaners a job". Though I am positive that was no reflection on the values of the school or the teachers and more of particular girls' parents. Unfortunately not being very politically minded in my youth, or used to questioning things and being a naive sponge, I didn't challenge things like that at the time, I probably even repeated such things. How I envy the people I've met since that had strong thoughtful opinions and were brave enough to voice them against the crowd.

The school could definitely have done with more emphasis on differing political viewpoints, it seemed completely absent from the curriculum. Though we were taught to be charitable and adopt grannies and suchlike, until the grannies were taken away from us too, for health and safety reasons.

Most of my school life occurred under the influence of Section 28 of the Local Government Act 1988. The section prohibited local authorities from "promoting" homosexuality or the teaching of "the acceptability of homosexuality as a pretended family relationship". With my Catholic upbringing I was pretty innocent, in fact I think I was quite old before I even realised gay people existed. If there were any gay people where I grew up, they must have been pretty discreet and disabled people tended to be hidden away too. There certainly wasn't anyone or any characters **openly** gay in mainstream media pre-watershed, that I can recall, until the Brookside kiss in 1994.

I do remember my more precocious sister asking my father how men had sex and I walked out of the room laughing at how silly she was, as men don't have sex together. So watching 'Wilde' in 1997 at Hull Screen art-house cinema was a bit of an education for me!

We had a gay teacher or two at my secondary school but they couldn't be open about it, no matter how many pink monogrammed shirts one of them wore. Apparently one teacher told my parents I would give him evil looks and seemed to view him with suspicion. Though I was probably still trying to work out exactly how gay men had sex. As it turned out, I don't dislike gay men at all, in fact I love them very much. As it happens, I lost my virginity to a gay man.

The Collection

I became pregnant whilst studying at University, the University of Lincolnshire and Humberside (a jumped up poly - as my mum liked to call it).

Although a talented painter, even if I do say so myself, I had become fascinated by photography at school. I used to take myself in on a Saturday to be taught black & white photography by a nice older gentlemen in one of the school's gorgeous Georgian buildings, then an empty disused boarding house.

One of the rooms had been converted to be a darkroom and although this was a club specifically for the boarders, sadly no one else attended. This was in 1994 and I was lucky that he was willing to continue the club, as we could have been putting ourselves in danger, him of false allegations and myself alone in the dark with an older gentleman. I don't remember his name but I am so grateful to him.

After school I went to The Kent Institute of Art & Design for a foundation course, where we were encouraged to try a bit of everything to see where our strengths lay. I chose to pursue work in the photography, video, performance and installation group.

That, in due course, led me to select Fine Arts with Time Based Media as a degree. I did not, at that stage, understand anything at all about the fact there were "good universities" and "not-so-good" ones. Some with great reputations for Art that I should really try to get into and ones that were, as my mum put it, jumped up polys. (Old polytechnical colleges converted into Universities - although I will add, where I actually attended used to be known as the Hull School of Art. - so that sounds slightly better.)

KIAD had tried to persuade me to stay on there, which would have been a good choice, if at the time I had wanted to remain in the vicinity of Kent. Had I made that decision at the time I was informed that it was not possible to get a student loan if your college/Uni was too close to home and I desperately needed to leave home and get away. I had also been persuaded that living in London would be hideously expensive so I didn't even consider any of the great colleges there. I went to visit Glasgow University which would have been amazing too, but decided it was probably a little too far away even for me. I narrowed my selection down to Sheffield and Hull.

Sheffield, because a previous student, Esa Evans, who now sells amazing jewellery under the name 'Lady Muck' in Whitstable, had returned to give us a talk which had really resonated with me. Sadly, they did not give me a place - I cried profusely, it was the first time I had been turned down for anything connected to my art.

(Unless you count the time I lost the art competition in Year 5 at primary and they chose the work of a boy which was far inferior to my masterpiece. My father reasoned with me that it was likely down to the fact I had copied a cat from a book and no matter how perfect it was, they were perhaps looking for something from the heart. Looking back now I think it was more likely because this boy was the naughtiest boy in the class and it was the only chance they had to praise him. Or maybe I am still bitter?

Talking of primary, it was also the first place I sold work. I had drawn a Snoopy and a girl called Anna offered me fifty pence for it! Please don't tell the Peanuts people. I was too young to know about copyright back then. Still, I think that was the first time I realised there was money to be made in making art.)

I came to accept the University rejection and realised it was for the best. Have you seen the number of hills in Sheffield? It's crazy. Hull was a flat plain as far as the eye could see, a good second choice. I don't regret going there as I made some good friends and had some great experiences. However, having a baby was not one of them!

I had terrible morning, afternoon and evening sickness and missed much of my second year. I was offered the opportunity to pass that year automatically due to extenuating circumstances, but stupidly chose to get through on merit with some extra time to catch up on work through the summer. Unfortunately due to the unforeseen personal circumstances of the tutor that made that offer, the official side of the paperwork went astray and as far as I know I never did pass that second year and have no record of the first. Although that never stopped me putting that I had a 'Certificate of Higher Education' on any future Curriculum Vitaes for job interviews!

My tutor had suggested that I continue my degree but I felt that having a baby should now mean giving up on my dreams. I thought that to be a good mother I had to be with my baby at all times and this didn't leave any room for my degree course. This is not a good idea, I don't recommend it. Though I found it depressingly restrictive, a baby is reasonably easy to handle in the first year and then it gets so much worse.

In more recent times I have come to the conclusion that Uni wasn't right for me anyway. I was so young, innocent and had little life experience and that led to a quite poor work. I recently read a quote from a Royal Academician that I would strongly agree with. He wrote that he would advise people to get a degree in a non-Arts subject, but something that interested them, whilst drawing, sketching and taking notes at night and then to take a post graduate Art course so that you could mix with the right people.

It took me to my thirty-fourth year to realize that my art wasn't just about my emotions and feelings like I'd first thought, but the common theme running through all of it was that of Psychology. And that if I ever were to return to a degree course, that would be the one I would choose. N.B. - you should choose a course that suits your interests, not mine!

In the following years I buried my desire for an art career. I had moved to Lancashire and after a year or so of running a failing hand-made card business purely to qualify for benefits (family credit) I tried to get a proper job to support my family. And yes I could have been on my own and received income support but that's just me, never one to do things the easy way. My first job was in a biscuit factory. The boss was nice enough, but on the shop floor I was bullied, I must have been too posh, or they were annoyed that I was taking their local jobs maybe? I had no ideas above my station and just wanted to make some money, but it was unbearable and I came home in tears and did not go back. It was also very distressing to deal with the punching in and out machines, which are demoralizing and inhumane in my opinion.

My next job was in a call centre which was only slightly better.

Whilst living in Nelson, Lancashire, I took my son on frequent trips to the library. I noticed that they had monthly displays of art and on one occasion I asked the library if I could book the reading room for an art display. They gave me a date a few months in advance but that was great because it gave me time to produce some work. I made a wall hanging, some photographs and some paintings. They were eclectic pieces. I noticed that the reading room was mainly used by Muslim men who went there to read Arabic papers. I'm not sure what they made of the manipulated photo of me jumping over the Nelson Mosque, but I certainly didn't make any sales.

Shortly after the Bradford and Burnley riots and the mini Nelson riot, I was starting to miss the village life I grew up in. There was also the fact that my son was starting to say words like 'castle' in a Lancashire accent that I had to consider - so I decided it was time to go home to Kent!

Seriously though, I missed home and returned to Kent in 2003, I think one of my reasons was to be nearer to my father who had been diagnosed with terminal cancer and we were told he had four years at best. Writing this in 2013 and he still refuses to die!

After a stint in a local supermarket, I got the best proper job I've had so far in my life, in the tax office. But I'm not allowed to talk about that or I'd have to kill you.

At some point in the duration of that job I figured out that I could take unpaid parental leave and took a month off to really concentrate on some painting. I took part in the South East Open Studios, an organisation that encourages artists to open their studios or homes to the public for two weeks every June. I exhibited my work in my house but it was really bizarre and not the kind of thing that would sell or make any money.

I had bought lots of wine for the opening day and may have written about this fact on a poster which only encouraged one man, clearly an alcoholic, who I could not get rid of, he stayed all afternoon and I had to keep hinting that it was kick out time. He rode off unsteadily into the sunset on his bicycle, not before telling me that his wife used to be a primary school teacher. I worked out she was the one who used to play piano for our music lesson and one day she lost it and shouted at me for always fidgeting with my hair in her class. I wasn't doing her any harm. I asked my mum to not go to school any more, she happily obliged by removing me and I was taught at home.

I took no pleasure in the fact that the woman who traumatised me in infancy was now living with such a man, no, not at all.

I left work to have my second child in 2005 and yet again suffered, or survived post-natal depression. In truth, and I never told the doctors this, I've had suicidal feelings since the age of seventeen and perhaps even earlier, but definitely seventeen as it is noted in my diaries. I think having a baby just made it worse. More intense and inescapable.

I remember one day feeling stuck, sat in an armchair in a dark and depressive mood. I could not move, the thought of moving was just exhausting. I was so unhappy. I decided then and there that I could no longer live a life, being servile to others, in such a way that made me unhappy. I felt I may as well be dead.

This is when I drew these pictures. I had started to draw myself out of depression. I was unable to draw or paint in any colour. It sounds strange but black on white (cream) was all I could manage. I think the fact that I couldn't use any colour was quite connected with my state of mind at the time.

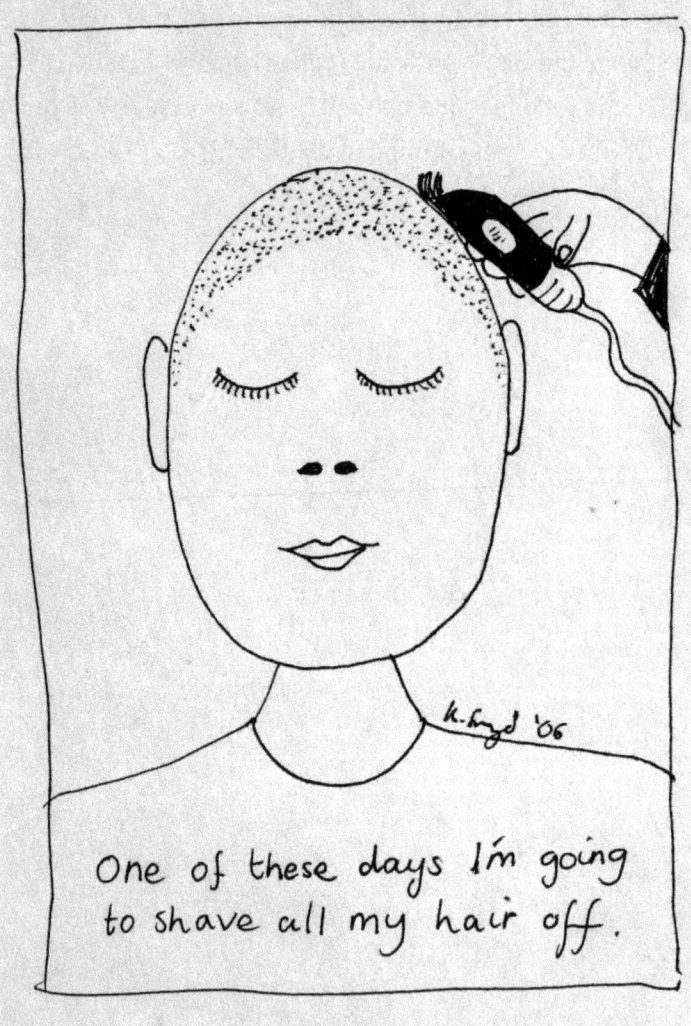

'Shave' 2006 Ink on Paper

Shave

I don't really remember the intensity of feeling like I had to shave my head. This picture reminds me how far away these feelings are now.

Apart from one time I've always had long hair, despite being pestered by girls at school to have a bob, especially when 'Rachel from Friends' haircut was all the rage. I did get my hair cut short many years later but the 'bob' did not suit me at all. My hair also has the propensity to be extra curly when straightened and straight when curled. I just can't win.

Anyway, I digress, I must have been feeling pretty bad to want to cut all my hair off but I can't think why I had the feeling, why I thought it would have helped my state of mind. And I didn't actually do it. Drawing the intention was enough. I suppose it would have been a cry for help. I was unable to care about anything very much at the time so perhaps I thought it would be a sign to others that I wasn't coping.

Not long after I drew this, Britney Spears shaved all her hair off, which caused a few shock-waves. Initial reports suggested she was having a breakdown but there were many other stories that might have been more likely.

- Quite recently I have again been attacked for my lack of hairstyle, by a relative-in-law type. Suggestions are a that a bob or a high but loose bun would be quite nice. Or at the very least some feathering around the front to shape the face a bit. Whilst I understand my lack of coiffeur-age can leave me looking a bit Alanis Morrisette-y from 1995, I guess I just don't care that much about what I look like. So, please take note before offering me hair advice. I'd rather paint a picture than spend time on my hair.

Having said that, I fully intend to make use of crazy coloured hair dyes and do some really funky stuff with my hair when it starts going grey.

Alternatively I will get into wearing wigs. I was recently mucking around with my mums wigs from the sixties and would really love to have a wardrobe full of wigs.

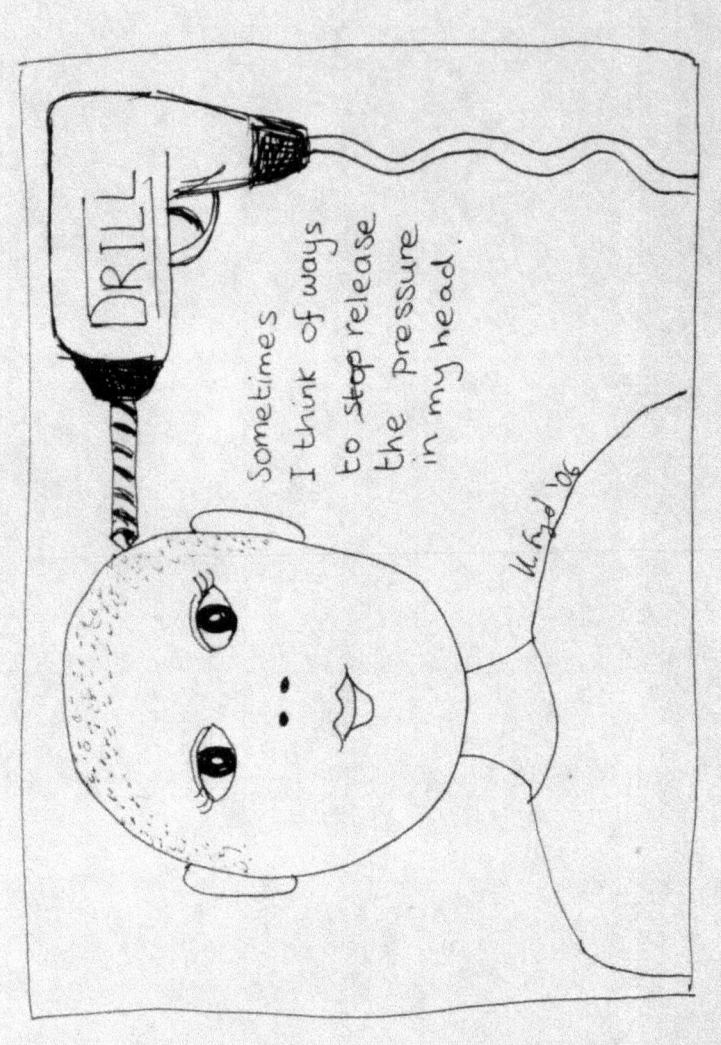

'Drill' 2006 Ink on Paper

Drill

I actually felt like this, I remember having such a terrible stress headache that I just wanted to drill into my head, it was only afterwards that I heard about the process of trepanning.

Not something I would actually advise people to do, but there are people who advocate this kind of thing. I am just interested that it was something that was in my head when I felt so bad, so I can see why others have sought it out.

My head felt so heavy, so pressurised. It was like the weight of the world was pressing down on my brain. Like a pressure cooker, it just needed a vent for the awfulness to escape.

And talking of drills - they are an essential part of an artist's bag of equipment, so get a good one. I still haven't.

It's okay when you are at college or University and you can summon a technician, but you really will need one at some point, especially if you are a painter and need to put up you own exhibition.

I inherited one from someone else's Grandfather and it is okay but I think it was made in the sixties and is corded so I need to drag a big extension cable around with me too. So I always have my eye out for a better, new and cordless one.

I usually carry all my equipment around in a rucksack suitable for hiking as I can't drive 'legally' yet. It's all a bit of a hassle and is one of the many reasons I have limited the number of exhibitions

I do now. They always have to be within the reaches of public transport.

Don't forget to purchase some masonry drill bits to go with the drill. And another essential purchase for the artist student are steel rulers. As one of my tutors once said and she was right, they are expensive but will last you your lifetime. So I spent some of the inheritance from my Granny on three of them, 300mm, 700mm and 1000mm. The rest of the small inheritance went on either food, clothes, partying or driving lessons whilst I was at college. I am not sure which. But I am glad I have something solid to remember my Granny by.

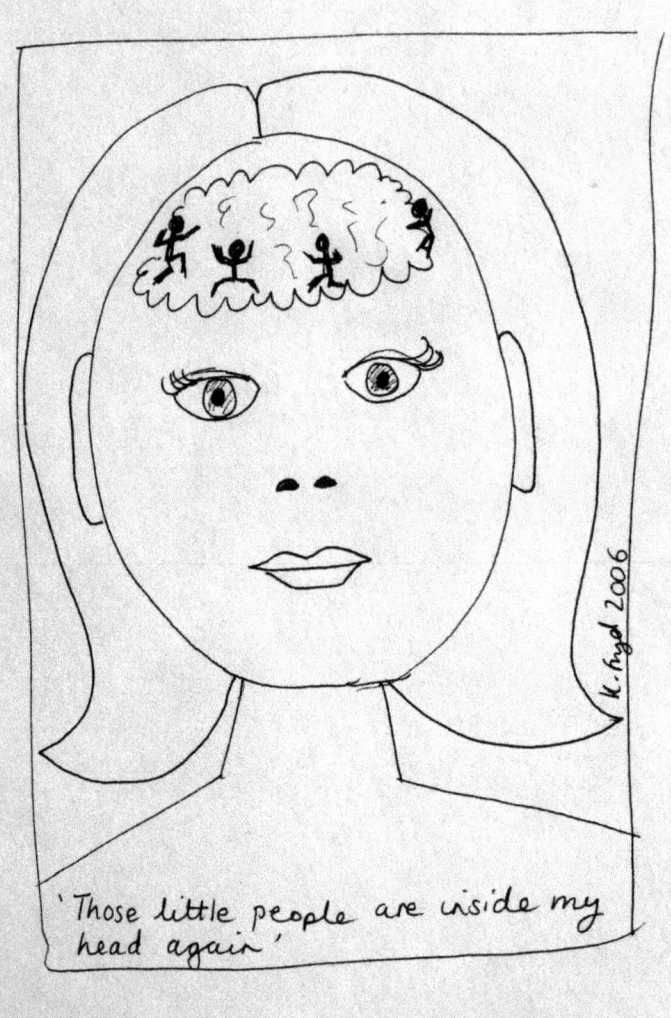

'Little People' 2006 Ink on Paper

Little People

In truth, I don't recall exactly the feelings I had in relation to this picture.

Perhaps it was all the thoughts running around my head. It could have been internal voices. It could also have been all the things to do that I had to remember, all the things people had said to me or the demands that were being made of me.

It's a shame that I can't remember exactly, but I suppose that means the viewer can come to their own conclusions about it. And those who have experienced it will empathise.

Some people might think that having voices in ones head is a little odd, but I don't think so. At least not in every case.

People should be able to express themselves verbally or pictorially, with whatever madnesses that they have in their minds. I think it can be more dangerous to keep it inside, not tell anyone, or be told they mustn't think a certain way. Although, once expressed, should sometimes be guided towards more healthier thinking.

Talking about suicide is one example. Talking about suicidal feelings is much healthier than not doing so. Having said that, I also realise, one of the most painful things in the world is hearing your child, friend or loved one say they that want to die - or seeing them self harm - yet I talk that way myself sometimes and can't seem to help it.

I'm lucky these occasions have reduced for me in recent times - and then one day it hits me again with full force. I welcome the feelings more, of late. I think "Hello sad or dark feelings, interesting that you are still here, I look forward to you going."

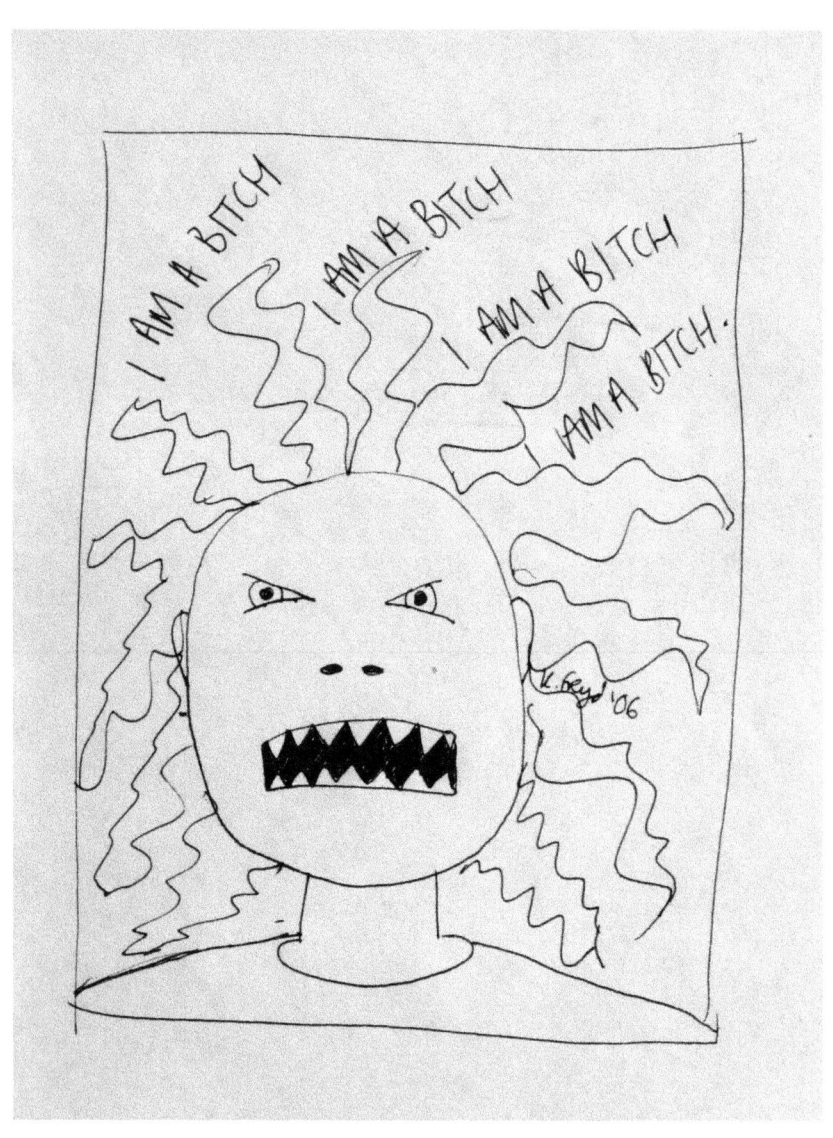

'I am a Bitch' 2006 Ink on Paper

I am a Bitch

I am the sweetest, calmest and gentlest being unless someone attacks me, physically or verbally. I am generally very patient, but I guess this picture represents what is called passive aggression. I bottle all the emotions up until I explode which looks a little like this.

Being tired and sleepy all the time after having a child, I was on the edge of this anger pretty much all of the time.

I am generally a conflict avoider and a people pleaser, a social chameleon. A two-faced bitch then? Yes, probably.

I am trying to learn the art of telling people how I feel at the time to save these sort of explosions. It is apparently a weakness, as people see you as crazy, your anger seems to have come out of nowhere, because the people treating you like dirt thought you liked being treated that way. They tend to be the manipulators.

Yes the manipulators spot a passive aggressive victim a mile off and team up with them for fun and games.

What makes me really angry is the way that people can take advantage of others who come forward as suffering from depression. This information can be used to discredit the ill person at any time in the future and it seems society is too easily persuaded to believe a person is delusional or violent. In truth the person may have only ever intended on harming themselves by cutting or suicide. There is therefore such a taboo about the subject of depression and sufferers learn to keep quiet about it, so that the manipulators don't take advantage.

As I have said before, it is always going to be more helpful to the sufferer to be able to talk about their feelings. Keeping all the emotions inside gives the dark thoughts a playground to expand in. Being allowed a safe environment to be able to express feelings is the key to getting help.

Now, whenever I hear of awful things happening in the world, I try not to be so judgemental and think that the person involved may have mental health issues causing their behaviour. I don't like to believe in pure evilness, that people are born that way. I think it's more likely that these people are victims of society.

I also find it interesting that some people who, when reacting to shockingly atrocious events and news stories showing up on social media, tend to write hideous comments themselves in reply. It seems to be okay for the outraged to voice their hatred and violence towards the clearly mentally ill, brainwashed or neglected in society, completely failing to see their reactions are not too far away from the thoughts of the initial perpetrators. Surely the only decent reaction can be the one born from love?

I know it's easy to say, I am not perfect. Lauren Sebastian, an artist friend of mine with a beautiful spirit, reminded me of this quote, which I think has it's origins in a Ghandi - We are only in control of being the change (or the love) we want to see - and I'm aware that there are people that I hate right now. It's easier for me when it's not personal! But I will strive to be that love.

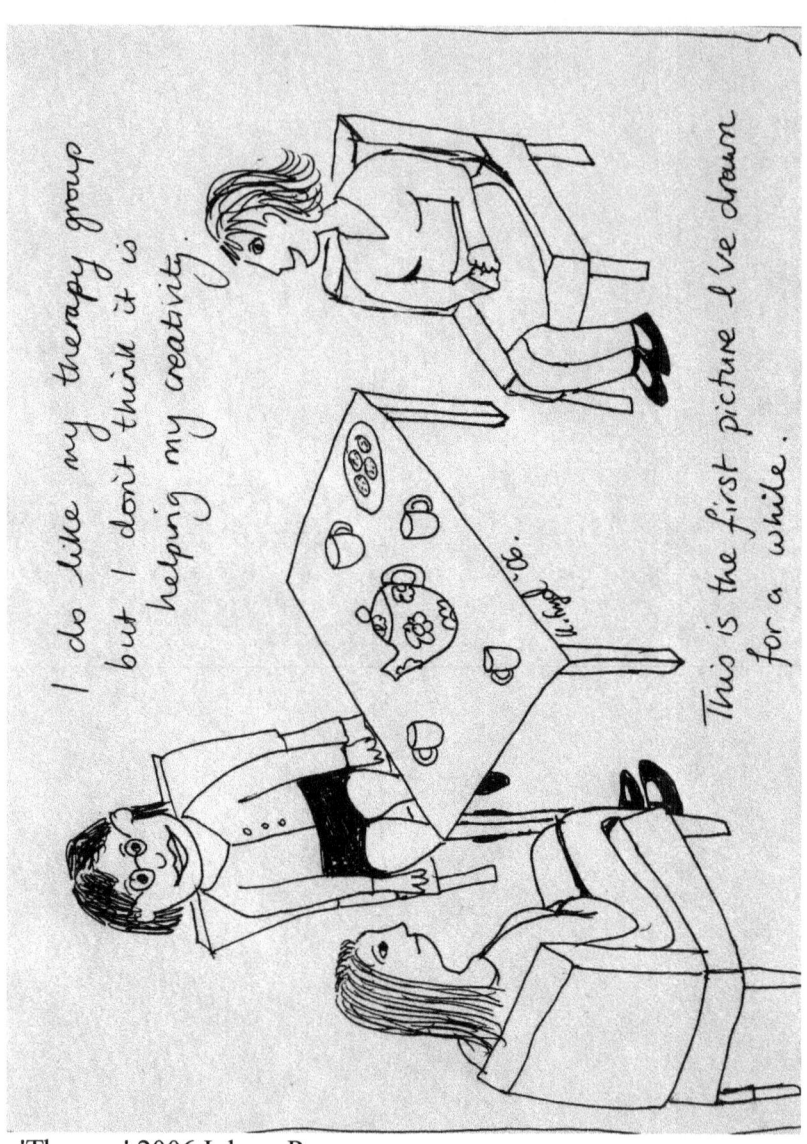

'Therapy' 2006 Ink on Paper

Therapy

I got post-natal depression after both of my children were born. I have many theories as to why this was. This picture depicts the therapy group that I went to, which was basically a load of depressed mums all getting together and talking about how miserable it is to have babies.

I imagine we all had other things wrong in our lives too. I said a couple of things which were obviously indicative of a craziness beyond the level that this group could deal with. Perhaps this group was just for the lonely. Anyway I was offered counselling because of something I said.

After a few weeks I think I managed to convince my counsellor that life was too short to do what we didn't love and she left the job to pursue more fun interests (or at least that is what I'd like to imagine she did?). In our last session she added that I could see a psychologist, should I want to. I did want to, but I didn't pursue it at that time. It was just another thing to add to my list of things to do. She seemed a bit exasperated with me after we'd decided at the last session that the key to start making progress was to get my daughter into nursery and I hadn't managed to do that yet. I did do that shortly afterwards though, and I did start to get better. I also think I do have her to thank for the break up of my marriage. But that was a positive thing.

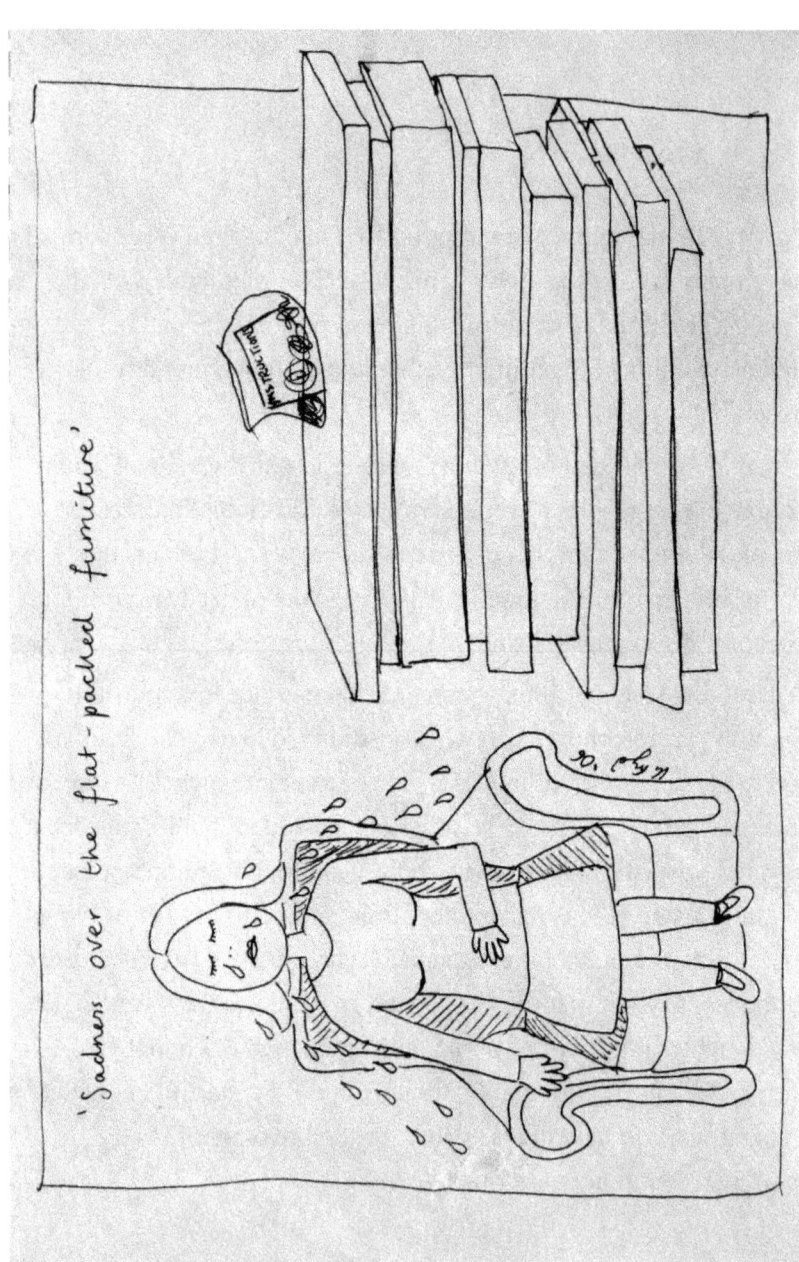

'Flat-packed Furniture' 2006 Ink on Paper

Flat-packed Furniture

As with any compulsive hoarder, there comes a time when you believe that if you can buy furniture to hide your hoard in, then you don't really have a problem.

So I trawled the internet for the best chest of drawers that I could buy for a bargain price and ended up finding a lovely piece of furniture from MFI. From past experience I had learned that you must never buy a flat packed chest of drawers, or one that didn't have dovetail joints. And definitely not ones with a flimsy base.

The day came when the furniture was to be delivered and when it did come, my error became clear. I swore that I had checked that this was one that came ready built but no, it was a flat pack. The delivery men piled up the planks of wood onto the space I had cleared for the brand new chest of drawers and left. I sat in a chair and bawled my eyes out.

I am a damn good flat packed furniture assembler, I'll have you know but this was not the point. I had to go through the farce of having the delivery drivers come back in a few days to pick the thing up again.

It was shortly after this that MFI went into administration. I think we can clearly see that the cause of this was entirely down to me returning this product. I will hold the guilt in my heart forever.

(When I was little I had a bad case of cystitis, this caused me to need a wee everywhere, including on one unamused girl's top, which she was wearing, as she gave me a piggy back ride. Another time, when I actually made it to a toilet, the toilet looked like it was in a bathroom, only the bathroom was in a big store. There is a possibility that store was also MFI.)

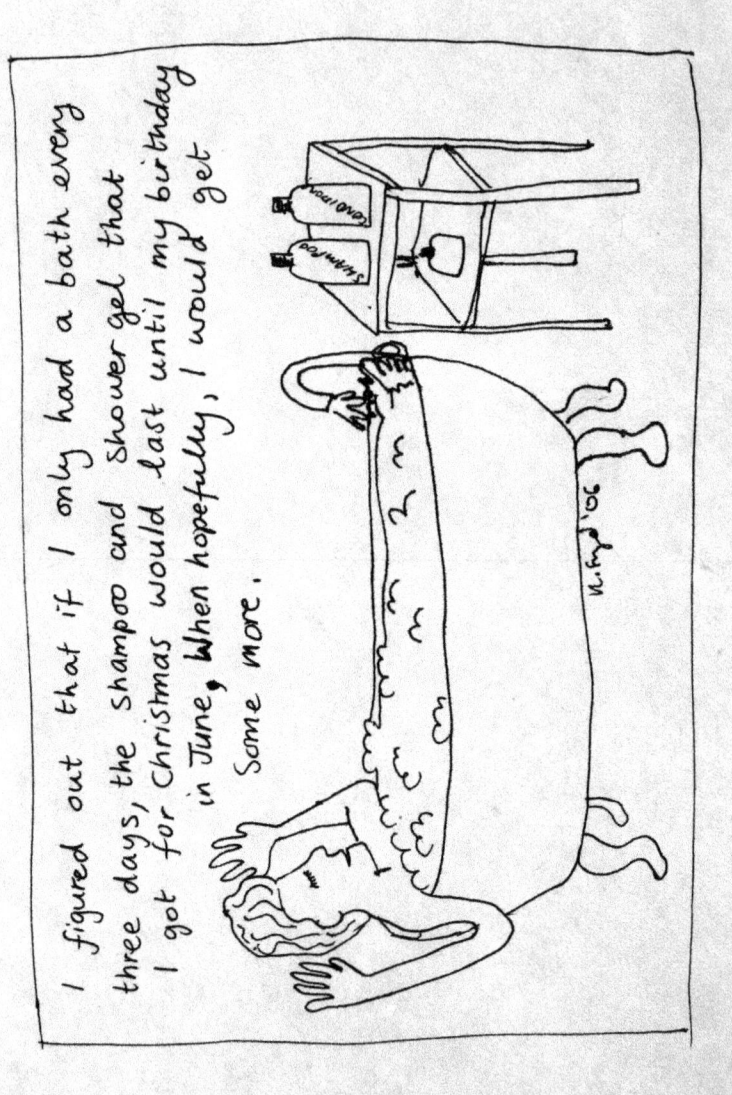

'Bath' 2006 Ink on Paper

Bath

This picture is basically true, I have been so poor that a gift of shampoo and shower gel was most welcome at many a birthday or Christmas time.

I think it is important for people to know that there are people living without basic essentials in the UK and that gifts of essential household products should be given more often, instead of plastic tat.

Generally, I do try to avoid washing anyway, as much as possible. My philosophy behind it is that there just isn't enough time for bathing in my life! I'm usually hiding out at home most of my time anyway, but will have a wash if it's a special occasion or I am meeting some people that day.

I have recently taken up exercising, so have started having showers again. It's such a pain.

But if I didn't have kids and could live self sufficiently for weeks at a time, I really don't think I would wash until I started offending myself with the whiffiness.

If you ever want to buy me a gift, shampoo and shower gel would still be happily received along with the other things I don't want to spend my money on, like kitchen and bathroom cleaning products. Especially the ones that you just pour down the toilet.

I try to only clean my toilet when there is a blue moon or when I have visitors. And I do my best to make sure that I don't have any visitors.

Maybe you readers could begin a new tradition at Christmas time - start leaving surprise packages of cleaning products and toiletries, all gift wrapped, on people's doorsteps and run away. I might do that when I grow rich.

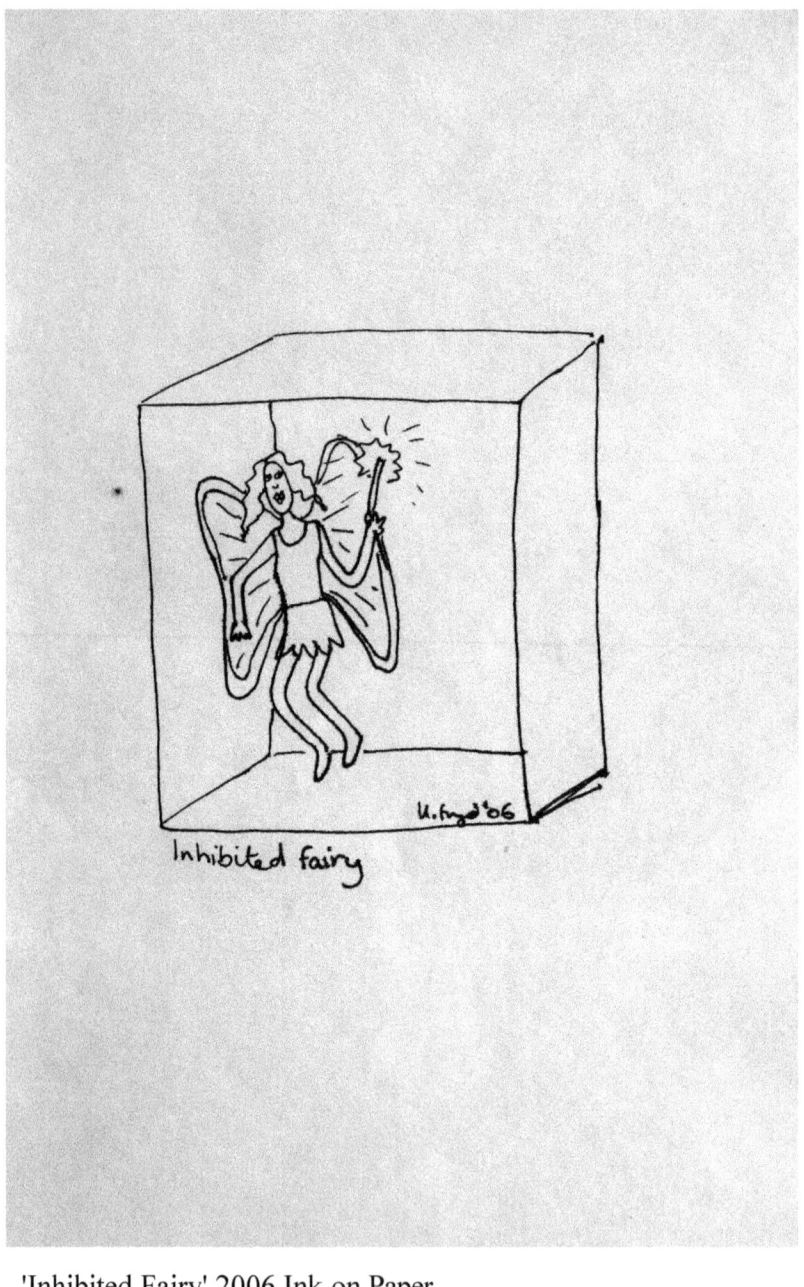

'Inhibited Fairy' 2006 Ink on Paper

Inhibited Fairy

Well inhibited fairy just says it all. I am in a box, stuck in a box and I can't get out and show the world just how fabulous and magical I really am. Part of this box was constructed by the relationship I was in at the time and partly by my children and my finances. But also my family and society. And maybe even just by me.

One time, when my baby was pretty new in the world, I had felt so boxed in by the four walls of my house, I felt like I couldn't breathe. I think there was probably an argument going on and I just decided to walk out, babe in arms, and kept walking until I could find some peace. I sat down by a pond a few minutes away, pleased to be breathing in the fresh air and having some peace and silence.

A little while later I was found. Apparently there was some concern expressed about the state of my mind and whether or not I would have hurt myself or my baby. I had no intention of anything like that at this stage.

Since having my own children though, I feel a little closer to understanding the actions of those mothers that do harm or kill their children. It is a mental health issue, but making it taboo for mothers to talk about it is not going to help anyone. I know some people reading this will know what I mean and others will think the idea is shocking and disgusting. I am certainly not saying it is right that anyone should harm or kill a child.

When I was at primary school I had a lovely teacher called Mrs Goody who taught us songs like 'She'll be Coming Round the Mountain', 'Puff the Magic Dragon' and 'Big Rock Candy Mountain', she taught us how to care for the school rabbits and she wore loose necked tops so that when she bent over to speak to us we could see her brassiere.

My naughty friend, Clare, "accidentally" allowed the male and female rabbit to get together, even though they were father and daughter bunnies, a relationship which is frowned upon in the Leporidae community. They had babies a month later and I remember Mrs Goody telling us to leave the babies alone and not even to peek at them as a mother can kill and eat her babies if feeling threatened or stressed.

When I felt depressed, I did want help, but I simultaneously wanted people to stay away. In the absence of love for my baby was an innate desire to protect. I felt that only I could keep him safe from any threats that were out there in the world.

I do not recall at any point in my pregnancy or soon after birth being given any advice with a strong emphasis on what to do about feelings that might surface that could cause immediate harm to myself or my child. Perhaps new mothers should be told what to do, just in case. Should they call 999 or self report to social services? Social services are in dire need of a massive re-branding though. Instead of feeling reassured that in asking for help, we will receive it, mothers are much more likely to fear that their child will be taken away from them. Therefore, in a mother's skewed mind, the thoughts maybe that the baby is surely better off staying in their arms. They are protecting their baby against all the dangers that could happen to them, even if it means taking their lives to do so.

[Due to a recent bad experience with the Social services I started to doubt that this service was actually of any help at all and nothing to do with the fear that can be associated with the name. I now see that some social care workers can and do abuse their powers and this should not reflect on the good people in the service. I believe I only just managed to avoid being arrested for murder by learning to say "no" when my instinct told me something wasn't right. Since then, I have been lucky enough to have undergone some intense therapy which has taught me that complaining in an official way is much better that punching someone to death.]

I understand those mothers who need to leave their children, their family and do their own thing. Us mothers are humans with our own needs and sometimes these needs are more important than motherhood. As I sat in my chair contemplating suicide, I weighed up the fact that my children and husband would have to carry on without me. In that moment, the realisation gave me the strength to see that any option was better than death. I could now allow myself to do anything I wanted without fear, as suicide was always going to be a worse option. Killing myself would be letting people down permanently.

I was and would still be a huge advocate of breastfeeding. But there are lots of problems surrounding breastfeeding. Being 'stuck' with a baby can become dangerously isolating for a mother, especially a new mother. So if you think you know someone who might be at risk, and you are able to, make sure you offer to take the babe for a walk or keep an eye on the babe while mum goes out. I don't think offering to help with the housework is as beneficial as taking the baby for a bit so the mum can do it herself. However, that could just be because I don't like people touching my stuff.

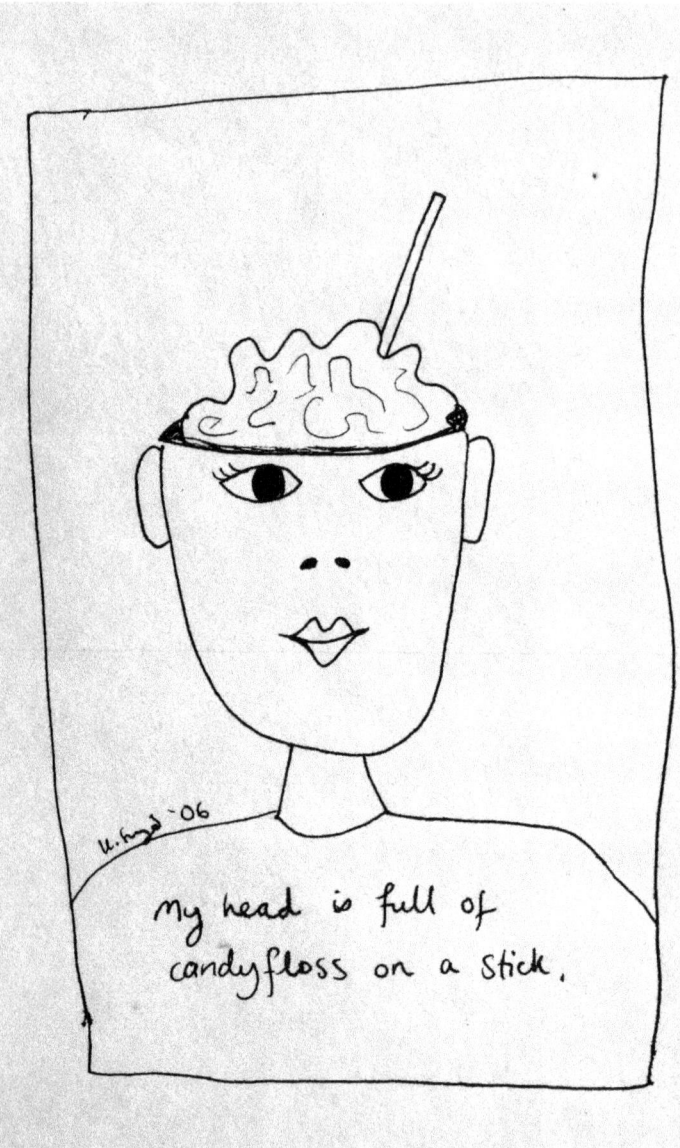

'Candy floss' 2006 Ink on Paper

Candy floss

Quite simply, my head was so foggy I couldn't think. Simple tasks became impossible.

I don't drive anything other than a scooter or a bicycle. So, at the time, because I lived half an hour's walk away from the centre of the village, I tried to plan everything that I needed to do, so that any task was was combined with one of the trips out to the primary school that my son was attending. That is what normal people would do, right?

I just couldn't handle it. I'd be late for school and I'd be completely flustered. The health visitor suggested I tried just taking my son to school and then to go straight back home and figure out what to do next. I didn't like this suggestion at all, but it turned out to be a life saver and something I still do today to keep me sane. Just don't give me any appointments before midday outside of the village.

I see many women juggling so much in their lives or at least acting 'busy'. I try to look at everything in an economic way. I like to think that by not running a car I can work less or at least work in the area that I want to work in and I don't need to rush around like a headless chicken trying to fit everything in. I can go about my life in a calm fashion at a pace I can cope with.

When I was seventeen I got a job in a family-run, local, mini supermarket. I must have been paid just over 23 an hour, and used to eat about 21 worth of snacks in my break. I earned about 230 a week and spent 240 a week on driving lessons.

It was a good lesson to learn, the value of money. As each horrible minute ticked by, I was adding up the cash earned in my head but it wasn't enough. I worked the unsociable hours of Friday and Saturday nights as my friends partied away. Without a job I wouldn't have been able to afford to do that anyway so it was catch 22.

This was before minimum wage came in. But let's face it, minimum wage is only any good for single people out there, it is no good at all for anyone with a family. We really need to see a move to a living wage.

I still can't work out the economics of the high-maintenance girls that I see wearing so much make up, fabulous hair and trendy clothes, working in high street stores on what must be close to minimum wage. I always think their clothes, hairdos and their make up must cost them more than they earn, therefore why work? They could be spending their time far more wisely. Are they living to work or working to live? Or in their cases, looking beautiful to work or working to look beautiful?

I always try and balance out the economics of working. After the supermarket, I once had a summer job picking cob nuts in Sutton Valence, just up the road from where I lived in Headcorn. It was piecework, so I didn't earn much at first. It took a while to get the hang of picking fast enough to get a good amount of pay. I had to get the bus to this job and as I was over sixteen I had to pay adult fare. After considering my bus fare I barely had anything spare in my wages. I also discovered that when the farmer decided we had picked enough, we had to stop. On one day I hadn't even earned my fare when the farmer found me and said, "Oh, didn't anyone call you? We're not picking today, so you will have to stop and go home."

It was a pleasantly monotonous job which enabled plenty of time to think of ideas, about love and creative endeavours. The job would have been okay, even with the ladybirds (that do bite) and earwigs that filled my dungarees, if it hadn't been for the limit on working hours. It only really seemed worth it for the workers who came from further afield and who had caravans, to sleep in, on site. I think I decided to stop doing this job after a couple of weeks. Not even the stories of Joanna Lumley stopping by to enjoy the fruits of our labour were enough to keep me coming back. Or perhaps we just ran out of nuts.

I'll always remember meeting a lad there, who got angry at me when I picked a flower for him. Confused by his anger, he proceeded to explain to me that to give a flower to someone is a lovely thought, but to leave a flower in the ground for them, is even lovelier. He was probably the first person I'd met with such strong opinions about the environment. But also a little curiously weird and obsessive about it.

As an artist, money and economics are such important issues and we have to learn to value our work. Both the artist and the hand-made craft person must consider this vital point. However, I have been guilty in the past of undervaluing my work, just to sell it, either to make some space in my studio or to help realise some necessary cash-flow. Pricing is a point of frustration for me. Whilst I have to consider what people will pay, there is little point working on a painting that works out to be earning me less than the minimum wage for the time spent on it, for example. It also needs to be considered that with all the extras an artist needs to do their job, one cannot base the price purely on the time spent on the work anyway.

Many people like to ask artists for freebies. It's such an odd thing. I can't imagine asking my friends to do a couple of hours of office work for me, for free. I also don't know whether people view artists as being able to sell their work for so little because the artist is doing something they enjoy or that appears easy or relaxing or whether it is because hobbyists can undercut the artists whose livelihood depends on a good price.

If I work out the cost of my time making the work and promoting myself, in addition to the materials, if I truly value my worth, the price becomes too expensive for many people. This is why I think we need products, such as prints and books, so that our work pays again and again. It is also helpful when selling to an interested and growing fan base, if we have products from the past ready to sell to them. Artists need to not be so snobby about selling posters and prints, all the major galleries are doing it!

One thing we do need to do, is really consider our market carefully. There are artists who make work with the primary intention of selling to the general public. Then, there are those whose work is not suitable for the same audience but whom have the ability to invoke delight in other artists and cultured beings. These are really two completely separate revenue streams and yet it is difficult for the artist, especially the painter, to see the possibilities of the latter without advice and guidance.

I am an artist, what do I spend my money on that other artists create? The answer to that question is what I need to focus on selling. I am one of the members of the market I want to sell to. Well, I tend not to buy art at the moment. I may do in the future but it is not on my current list of things I need. However I am keen on reading and looking at other artists work, especially the successful ones. So books and similar products are a good sell for the artist with the more alternative work. Sometimes you are lucky and your art is interesting to both other artists and the general public.

Many people have suggested to me the places where I should sell my work: cafés, restaurants and suchlike. My reply is usually that they are not really suitable venues considering some of the subjects I cover and I struggle endlessly about what kind of artist I am. I think at heart I am the type of artist for other artists to admire and for the time being, my work will suit books and exhibitions where I can make a point about an issue that I am interested in.

I am extremely stubborn and am not really interested in spending time making things for other people. I want to make work that I am fascinated by and if I find some other people that are fascinated by it too, then that is great. However, as a painter, I do sometimes find myself distracted into the pursuit of finding a subject that sells, to support my other endeavours. This is especially difficult not to slip into when your main way of communicating is through the medium of paint. Does a sound artist start making mainstream sounds to sell? It is also extremely hard not to fall into the role of the artist for the masses, when you are trying to support and bring up a family.

Having had a variety of shitty jobs in my life, I then spent a vast amount of time on benefits of one kind or another. My childless friends do not really understand this lifestyle choice. So I will try to explain.

I spent the children's early years working full time and for two and a half years ended up getting 2100 into debt for each month I worked and that was living really basically without any luxuries. I put this down to train fares, the private house rental prices in the south (and lack of social housing) and being under-qualified for anything that paid a living wage. It's all very well people getting snooty about the lazy benefit people but when you know your family will be worse off with you working and you never even get to see them, sometimes you are more sensible to work the system within the rules.

I'm not talking about benefit cheats. Benefit cheats and those with jobs who claim unemployment just cause trouble for the innocent. They deserve to be punished, although it would be nice to see them punished fairly and proportionally to the tax evaders.

The propaganda media would have you believe all those relying on state hand outs are lazy-work-shy-beer-swilling-television-watching-breast-enlarged-good-for-nothing-scumbags, and that there are millions of them. In reality, there are very few people who really don't want to work. I've spoken to many people who love working and wouldn't want it any other way. So if so many are keen on working, does it really matter that a few wish not to and would rather *choose* to live a life in miserable poverty?

If this still really bothers you then you can always make it your life's mission to inspire them back to work rather than punishing them by shoving your disgust down their throats.

I am certainly not work shy at all, it's just that I don't see why I should struggle doing a menial job with rubbish pay that is going nowhere just because nature gave me a uterus and I made some unwise decisions a very long time ago. I have to at least hope that there is an end to the misery of poverty. If I had to think this was my life script then I might as well end it now!

I'm not saying that people should never do any crap jobs, I think it's a good idea for everyone to do something pretty awful for a few years. Like a rite of passage, to learn the value of money and how to treat people who work in service industries for the rest of your life. You've got a good lot of kids coming out of school each year that are used to being treated badly, who won't find working conditions quite so terrible and who get to spend all their wages solely on themselves rather than their partners and their children. When they wise up, they can move on. Once you get older or have a family to support it's much harder to accept the mistreatment and the poor wages. While I'm on the subject, why don't teachers and carers get paid more? Amazingly important work not paid properly and therefore not attracting the best.

I actually work really hard for many hours a week. It's just that what I do has not been remunerated enough thus far. I await the respect due when it does. It does seem as though the general public think a good novel is just pulled out of the author's backside at will. No thought to the years of work and crafting their technique is ever given. It appears as if by magic, similar to all creations, be it art or music and so on.

So why is it so difficult to make a living as an artist? Is the spectacle of the select few artists making it to the top, just created to boost the economy of the profitable hobbyist art trade? Why does the joke of the poor artist and the artist only making money in death still exist? Partly this is down to the secrecy of the art world and how it works. This is why there are some artists at the top making millions and others thinking ... but how? And so many artists at the top seem to keep the secrets of how they did it to themselves. Or could it be because a certain amount of luck and "who you know" was involved, and you can't pass that information on.

If I discover the secrets I intend to share them willy-nilly. I have already set up online social media and video sharing sites under the name 'Katy Fryd - How to Be a Successful Artist', to share any advice that I have picked up thus far.

Many quotes for struggling artists float around the internet and also come from interviews with people that are apparently successful, saying, "Work hard", "Never give up and you will get there", "others will give up and you have to remain in the game". This is not good enough advice on it's own. It suggests you have to wait for others to fall in love, want families and mortgages and they will fall by the wayside into dull but regular jobs and eventually because you've been hanging on for dear life, you will be noticed? I don't think so. I think every artist needs a strategy.

I have a paranoia that tells me being an artist is considered not suffering enough. Instead of the majority of society being kind and supporting one another, many seem selfish and want to see others doing worse than they are. Or at least, having a tougher life.

Being a single mother, an artist and surviving on benefits is not being punished enough for being alive. One must take a menial job for life to be fair to those hard workers, apparently. Oh, unless you were lucky enough to be born with a large trust fund. What about the fact that this is my vocation and give me the chance to be one of the best and I will be. I will earn lots of money and be able to pay huge amounts of tax. Which I will pay, by the way, not hide off-shore.

If you are on benefits, you tend to be the lowest of the low, living day to day, not knowing if you are going to be able to pay the next bill that comes in. Those that complain about the benefits claimants tend to have reasonable jobs and they will have cash to spend on enjoying themselves and doing fun activities. Most of those lucky people will also be paying towards a mortgage so that at some point in their lives they will be able to pay it off and own their own property. Benefits claimants will never be able to do this.

With my dire level of qualifications and earn-able level of income it's no wonder why I see my options as being that I can either try my hardest to reach for my goal and if it works I may also be able to own my own house one day. Or be subjected to a life of misery in a job I can't stand, to work all the hours God sends and have no extra time or enjoyment to life *and* still not be able to save a big enough deposit to get my own place one day - and then I will die!

There is, of course, the option to retrain but going to University nowadays is such a costly affair. I'll be paying back my loans forever.

If I ruled the land I would like to decree that everyone receive their own place to live in at a certain age in adulthood. Basic but livable in. The government no doubt fears this would stop people from working or grind the housing market into the ground (no bad thing!) but I don't think that would be the case. It would however mean a lot less stressed and unhealthy people walking around.

When will people realise, (and by people, I mean the government), that artists can actually boost an economy. They are the creators of products that can make more money and therefore taxable income for their country. Artists, who would be that much more productive if they didn't have to worry about money. This country needs to look at other countries who pay artists a small income to do their thing. Every so often, out of that, amazing creations will appear. There would not be a danger of everyone choosing an art career because they were too lazy to work, as it would only need to be a minimal income such as benefits are now.

I actually think Universal Credits is a good idea in theory. The current system of Tax Credits is fine, it's the Housing Benefit system that is flawed, always has been and always will be. At the moment there is little point for a person who needs housing benefit to earn anything over breaking even, if at the end of all the calculations, they are still in receipt of some of that benefit. This tends to occur if you have a big family, are renting privately in the south and are on a low income.

The plus side to working is that the nosey neighbours are not gossiping about you being an unemployed waster and therefore gaining a bit of self worth, which doesn't add up to much if you find you are getting into debt. Current housing benefit and council tax legislation takes away pretty much all support if you start making a profit or have an income from a job. Yet with

PAYE work you have additional deductions such as travel and smart clothing costs and unless you are very handy at making pack lunches - food costs too. (It seems strange to say making lunches at home is a hassle - the time and anxiety involved in these things appears to bother me. This may be because I have mother duties too. I am sure if I lived on my own this wouldn't be an issue. But often, flying out the door with a few seconds to catch a train, means buying lunch is simpler.)

The problem with self-employment is that the unhappy mixture of tax credits and housing benefit can cause problems for the artist that does not have a guaranteed regular income. Future years of benefit income can then be calculated based on the fact you earned a lot in one particular year and yet housing benefit is not as flexible as tax credits so the result could be months of not having any money to pay your rent.

However, Universal Credits will come with their own problems for the self employed. There is talk of monthly account filing. To me, this just means extra paperwork. This will be terrible news for the creative, the artist or writer, who may make quite a bit of money at one time of the year and not at others. Combining that with the idea of an expected income floor for the self employed based on the minimum wage, it is going to be hellish. If income is not balanced out over the entire year, creative people are going to end up really struggling. Unless I have not quite understood exactly what is going to happen, which is not surprising as there has been little information given, I think it might be easier, horror of horrors, for artists to sign on and maybe take a normal PAYE job if they haven't figured out a way to make a regular income by the time Universal Credits kicks in.

It seems to me that the government do not want to allow a system where creative people can thrive, they want to create an army of workers. It is a very short sighted view. Think of all those amazing books not being written and all those masterpieces not being painted. The only benefit is that the truly determined will still get through whatever barriers are put up, as long as crippling depression doesn't get to them first.

The only other option is to try and earn so much money that you don't need to go near the benefits system with a barge pole. Creative types might need to consider a mass exodus to cheaper places like the north or Wales.

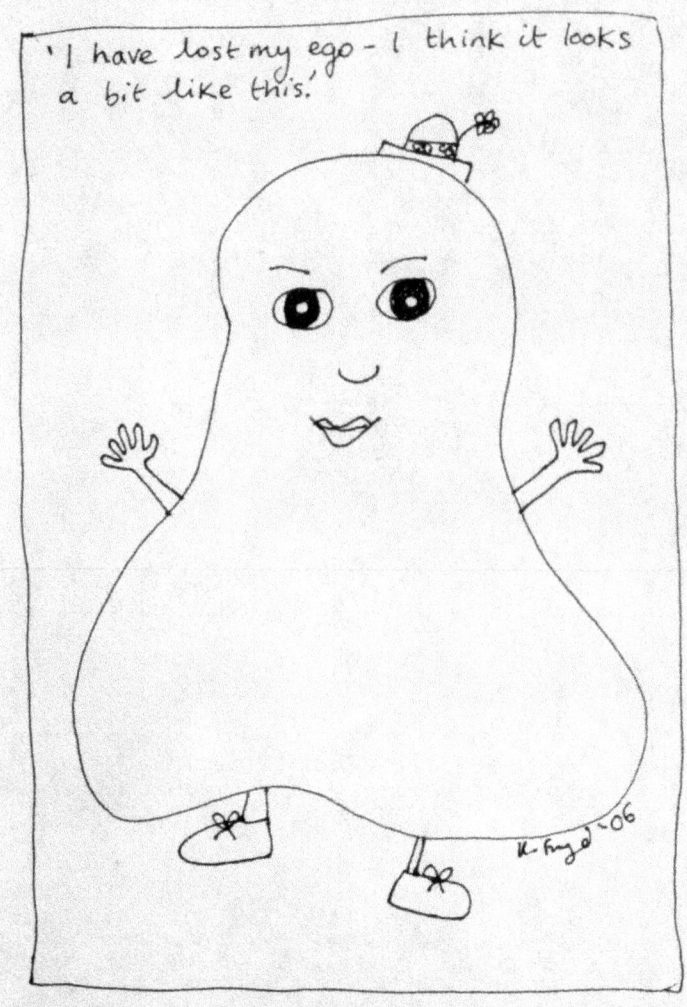

'Ego' 2006 Ink on Paper

Ego

People have said to me that this image represents the wrong use of ego but I am talking about the ego defined in Sigmund Freud's structural model of the psyche, the function that stops people from saying the wrong thing, that makes them behave correctly. I did and have still lost mine. It is like the on/off switch for my ego got tampered with. The part of my mind guiding me between what I want to do or say and what I have learnt I shouldn't do or say, was faulty. This is the voice that listens to the rules for social normalcy and decides you won't do that particular thing because it will cause you embarrassment. Well, my switch got damaged during this period of depression and has never been fully restored.

When I drew my ego it ended up looking a bit blobby with a hat, I am not sure why.

I have found that losing one's ego is good for shouting at boys who are setting off fireworks in the park.

But losing one's ego, a little bit, is useful for an artist. You have to learn not to care about what other people will think of you when you make your art. Otherwise you will end up only making safe work. Artists may well need to make a fool of themselves or take their clothes off or do a piece of work based on secrets or feelings. (n.b. You don't really need to take your clothes off, although it has been known to help artists get noticed in some cases.)

You have to believe in yourself and have confidence. If you are starting out thinking that you want to reach the level of a well respected, world renowned artist - well that artist wasn't born that way. He was either raised with the greatest gift of a huge amount of confidence and esteem which he willingly accepted or he made the decision to be that person at some stage in his life. He accepted the accolades and the respect that people gave him.

I've always felt that I am a great artist and that my work should be famous. It is only the reality of being unknown or undiscovered that causes a rift with that thought. I have to be that great artist to others. I have to put myself up on that pedestal to be respected. And if you are a budding artist you will have to be prepared to do that too. Obviously it helps if you achieve something amazing. I'm just saying don't wait for someone else to tell you what you are doing is great. If you believe in what you do and have integrity that is enough.

I understand it is very hard to do. I am doing it right now, by writing this book.

I had a wobble when I wrote my first book, a kid's book, called The Cat Inspector. It was self published, yet people were asking me to autograph the book and I felt like a fraud. I wasn't quite ready to put myself on that pedestal. Being published by an established press is just a real voice telling you what you need to hear, telling you that your work is good enough and that you have achieved acceptability from an outside source. You've then got your recommendation, your review and your confidence that you can trade on. But guess what - you don't need that external voice if you just believe in yourself.

And you know what - you've got to believe in yourself! If you don't, you can be sure as hell no one else is going to do it for you! You will, in fact, find quite the opposite is the case, most people will be all too ready to jump in with negative comments. Just remember that we were all born with talents and gifts and we have to allow ourselves to shine to be the best we can be, in our own profession.

We must consider that when death takes away everything, nothing really matters any more, therefore surely the best thing we can do when alive is to make life more enjoyable and bearable for others, using our unique gifts and talents. This is the same for any profession, from a doctor, a scientist, to an artist or comedian. I therefore decree - this is the meaning of life!

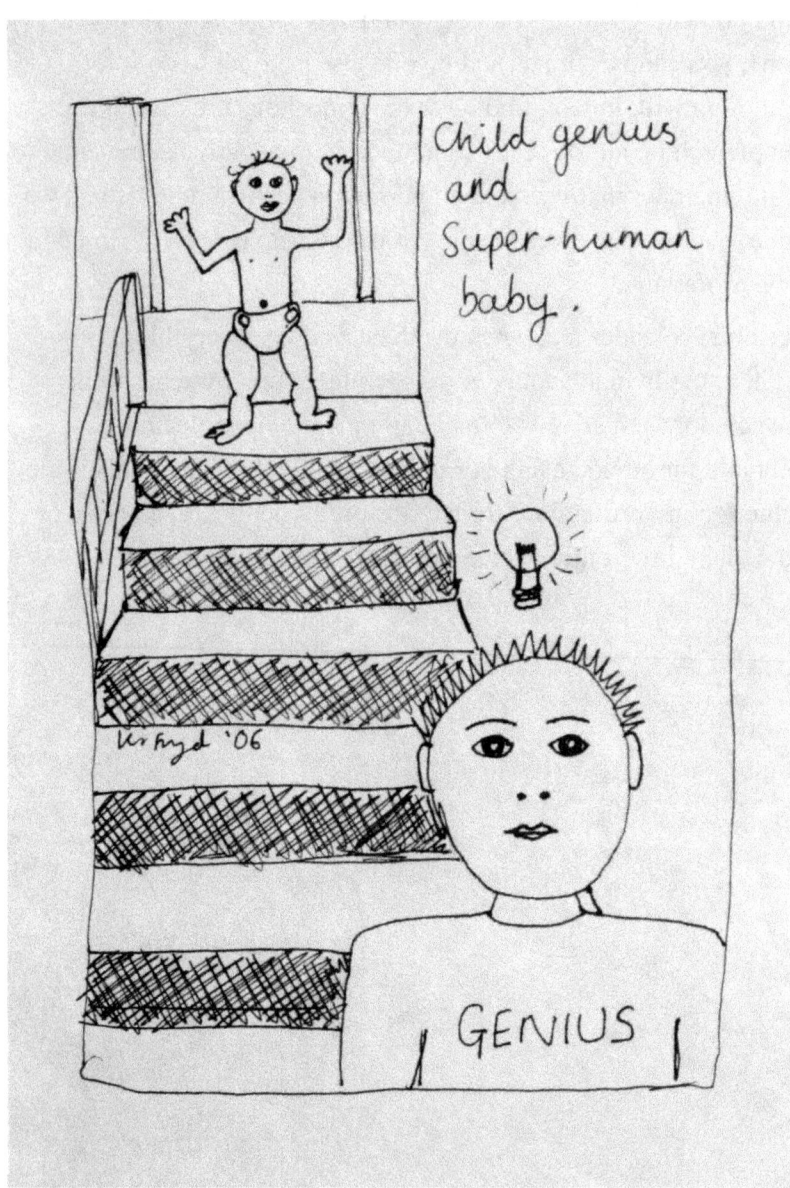

'Genius Child' 2006 Ink on Paper

Genius Child

Ah now, this reminds me of the time when I had a young baby and had regular visits from the health visitor due to my depression. Who, with my permission, had told my elder child's school about my illness. In reply, she had been told that I had been complaining to the school about my child's progress as they had labelled him as 'average ability' and I had disagreed. She said there is nothing wrong with being average, and I said that I agreed. There is nothing wrong with being average if you ARE average, but if you are very intelligent and being labelled as average, then that is a significant issue. She looked at me as though I was mad and thought my child was a genius. (He is of course.) Several years later my son passed the equivalent of the 11+ and got accepted to grammar school without any tutoring from outside sources. Who's the crazy fool now? Parents - always believe your intuition.

The very same health visitor once saw my 9 month old daughter climb the stairs with great agility, without me immediately behind her. This upset the lady who exclaimed that she had not seen the like in twenty years of working as a health visitor. I said that was because she had never met my daughter. She kept going on about how I should be right behind her in case she falls. And in the end I called my husband down from upstairs, to help me argue my point. My husband being of weedy frame was not likely to start any physical fights but she suddenly exited the house faster than you can say Jack Robinson. I hate to say I found this amusing as she was certainly not under any threat from us, but I guess she had been trained to just get out in these situations.

Much later on I discovered a tree close to Rochester castle which was covered in tags with names and job descriptions on it. It soon became clear they were all health professionals that had been killed in the line of duty.

I still believe if a baby were to fall on the stairs they would no doubt do a lot less damage to themselves than an adult falling down them. As my daughter got older she thought it was great fun to slide down the stairs on her belly - still not quite sure how she achieved it.

Whereas, I did take a tumble down the stairs once and I thought I was going to die. I was reaching for something the wrong side of the stair-gate at the top of the stairs when I did a cartwheel over it and landed in a heap at the bottom, entangled in two stair-gates. As I tumbled, my life flashed before my eyes, and honestly all I thought was, "Great, is this it?!" My entire life was about to end in an instant and I'd done nothing with it.

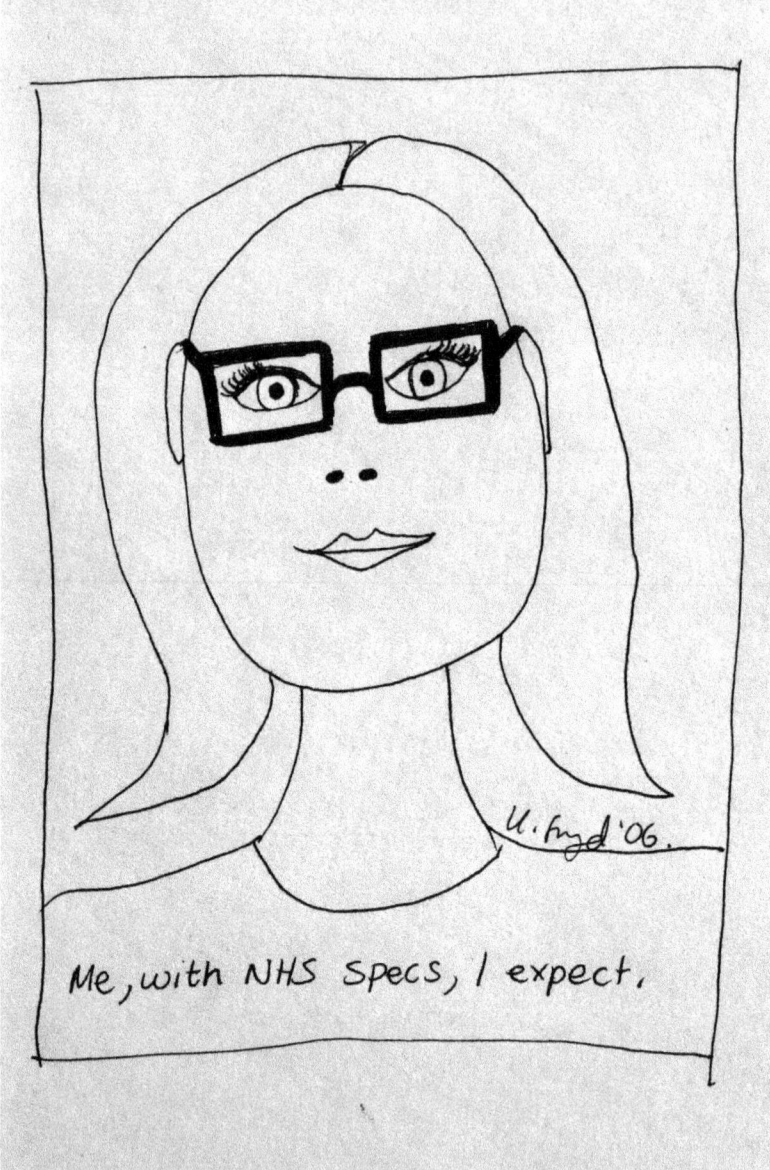

Me, with NHS specs, I expect.

'NHS Specs' 2006 Ink on Paper

NHS Specs

NHS glasses are the bane of my life. I remember the first ones I ever got at the age of five. Clear plastic, thick rimmed, granny looking things. They would probably be trendy now, quite retro. I hated them and would hide them from friends in class and thought they couldn't see with my special stealth glasses move. It made me really good at memorizing sequences of letters from the blackboard and probably spellings too, now I think about it.

As my eyesight diminished I got through several pairs of glasses. Another memorable pair was the pair I had at about thirteen. By then I was fed up with the arms of glasses going out of shape all the time and falling of my face or slipping, and was impressed with a pair that had better arm engineering. It felt like it had some powerful elastic in the hinges. I have just searched on the internet for 'elastic hinges for glasses' and there are a huge number of patents, it's obviously big business.

These particular ones were dark grey and large 'Deidre Barlow' style. Though I hadn't heard of her at that time. Soaps were largely frowned upon in our family home and thankfully most likely in the houses of the children who attended the posh school I went to. So I didn't get bullied, for that anyway - or if I did, it went over my head. If only I had been a teenager nowadays I would have been the one trend-setting the geek-chic fashion.

My mother told me these glasses looked good on me, and she stands by that comment to this day. Personally, I think she made it her mission to keep me as ugly as possible for as long as possible to keep the boys away!

When I was fifteen I was allowed contact lenses. Oh joy! Oh happy day! Of course, it wasn't for reasons of vanity, it was because I was so sick of my glasses getting rained on and steaming up as soon as I entered houses. At least, that is what I told my mother.

I had been ugly for so long, with my buck teeth, glasses and skinny frame. I transformed like a geek girl from one of those teen, 'ugly pretty girl' movies, literally overnight (bad-usage-of-literally-irony), to a more voluptuous, braces being removed straight toothed, glasses free bombshell. Well that's how I remember it anyway! The only problem was, I still had the self esteem level of ugly and unworthy which was probably to blame for the poor choices of boyfriends I made in later life. I have become aware of other reasons that may have caused my feelings of unworthiness, but I am not ready to talk about that yet.

One problem I've had with glasses is that they have never, ever suited me. I look so stupid in them. Lots of people look great in glasses, but I wasn't blessed with the right shaped face for that at all, and now I am a bit porkier, they look even worse. As I am still living life with a minimalist income, until of course this book takes off and I make my first millions, you'll still find me purchasing the cheapest possible glasses, as they are so ridiculously expensive. When I've made my initial million, my first purchase will be of a pair of glasses with the best hinge elastic technology of the day.

I am glad they can thin the lenses down a bit now, as my eyesight was so bad the glasses used to be incredibly heavy. But, hang on, what is this newfangled scratch-resistant technology? - No, thank you very much. I will tell you now, scratch resistant just means I am likely to scratch them a lot more. So I will ask for none of that fancy stuff nowadays. I want to be able to rub my eye glasses on my t-shirt.

[Disclaimer: I visited the opticians after writing this bit and the assistant told me it might not be the scratch resistant coating that I am talking about but the reflection-free coating. Also she said the coatings have improved over the years and may not be as bad as the pair I had previously.

She added that I really shouldn't rub them on my t-shirt or get soap on them. Soap - Aha! Was this the problem? I wear my glasses in the shower (on the rare occasion that I wash) and of course the shampoo would have got on them and ruined them.

One chap at University used to tease me for wearing my glasses in the shower as he always removed his (p.s. we were not showering together). He could not understand why I would wish to keep mine on. I don't know whether he thought I liked to wear them so I could take pleasure in seeing myself naked in 20:20 vision or what? I didn't think it was that unbelievable, I just wanted to be able to see clearly whilst washing. I hate any reminder of my severely myopic prescription.]

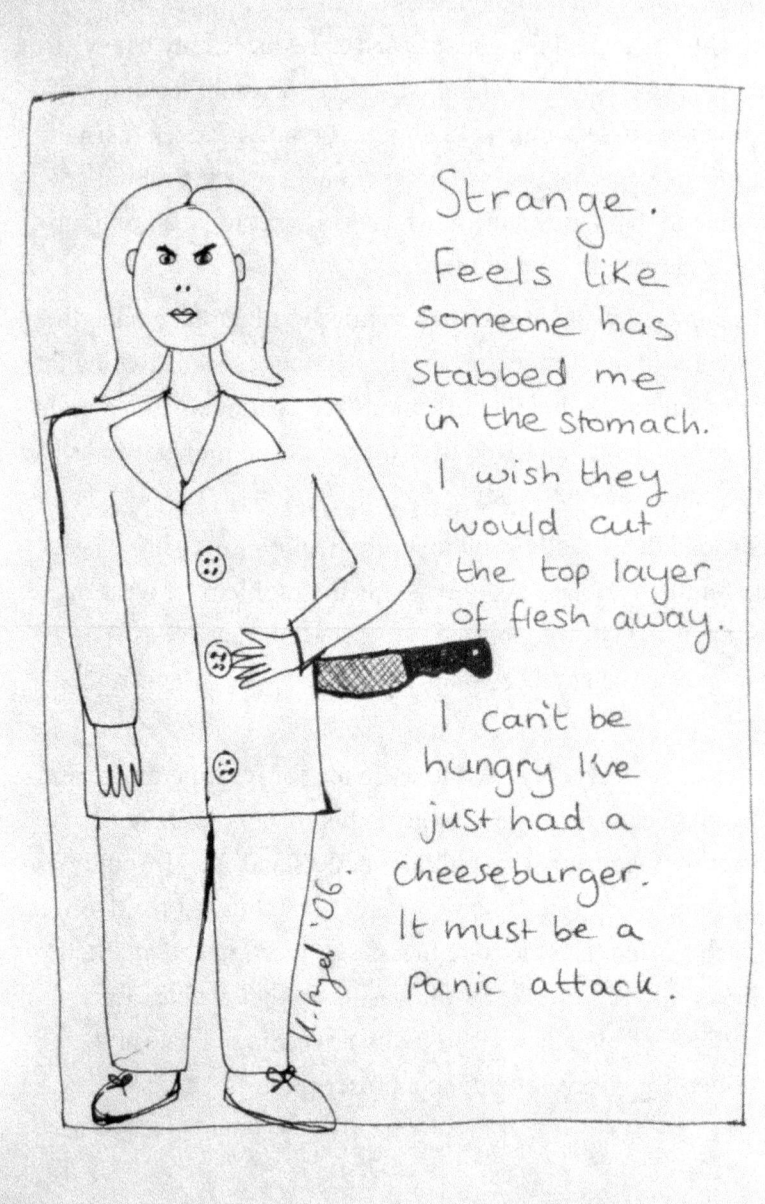

'Cheeseburger' 2006 Ink on Paper

Cheeseburger

My baby was attached to me, non stop. Have you ever had that
feeling when you go out without your handbag? Well going
out without your baby is a little like that, at first.

Also after being inside the house for a long time, any exposure to
the outside world is a bit of an eye opener. I would say like an
acid trip, though I've never been on one. But definitely a bit like
the first time I took codeine and everything became more defined
and coming toward me in high definition 3D.

This picture is clearly about a panic attack, the likes of which I
have luckily forgotten. I still don't particularly like crowds, they
make me a little anxious but this picture shows that I was
experiencing real pain. So I must have been pretty terrified. I
suppose it's a bit like a kid who gets tummy-ache when they are
afraid to go to school.

I remember exactly where I was though. I was in Ashford in
Kent, walking towards the train station from the Designer Outlet
Shops, with it's huge marquee type roof.

Funny how a picture can transport us back in time. So here's
another thing you can try if you've never done it before. Sketch a
picture a day in a dedicated sketchbook. It turns into a visual
diary. And if you don't want to sketch, try a photo a day. It's
good practice to keep a camera on you at all times anyway. I've
just realised, that sounds old fashioned, as most people have

cameras on their phones these days. I don't use the one on my phone. I like to have different devices for different objectives.

It was always much more fun to use a film than it is to use digital. That way you have time to forget what you have taken and you get a pleasant surprise when you get them developed. I have about 6 rolls of film that are currently waiting to be developed from about 5 years ago. I think one has a picture of a naked man's bum on it - can't wait to see that again!

Conclusion

After making this work I made some further pen drawings which moved away from the subject of depression to the subject of things I found amusing in my life. Pictures that were given a twist of black comedy.

After that, I started painting again, in colour! First of all I used pastel colours and then they got a lot more vibrant and I haven't looked back. My pictures had also developed a strong sense of style. And I even painted a more realistic portrait, more recently, which would have been impossible in 2006.

So my point is, if you are an artist who lives with depression and you're feeling blue and struggling to make any artwork, just start. Right now, pick up a pen, just start drawing on some paper. If you don't have any paper, draw on this book. Or you could give this book to a friend if you think they might enjoy it. Actually scratch that, draw on this book and purchase another one as a gift for a friend. I have to get to that first million somehow.

You might not get the masterpieces straight away but they will come. Otherwise, the most fantastic pieces will never be seen if they stay inside your head and that is no good to man nor beast.

What you have to say is unique and valid, as there is no other person on this planet with your individual perspective.

Go forth and let your work multiply!

- the great Katy Fryd has spoken.

Important things you have learned from this book which made it worth buying:

- The number one rule is, there ain't no rules!
- Document! Document! Document!
- Choose a University with a good reputation.
- Do not go to Sheffield unless you are keen on hill- walking or need to tighten up your calf muscles.
- Do not get pregnant or have children - EVER!
- Do not go straight to University to study for an art degree if you've had a relatively middle class upbringing.
- Get a degree in a non arts subject and then do a post- graduate course in an Art subject.
- Do not get a job in a biscuit factory if you have trouble completing simple repetitive tasks involving a conveyor belt or have a posh voice.
- Do not try trepanning. The likelihood is that you will not survive.
- Do buy yourself a strong cordless drill, masonry drill bits, and steel rulers.
- Do not buy a flat packed chest of drawers.
- Always make sure drawer fronts have dove-tail joints when making a purchase of anything with a drawer.
- Keeping yourself clean is wasting precious time in your life that could be spent creating.
- Always offer to give new mothers some breathing space.
- Do not try to do too much and burn yourself out.
- Do not buy glasses with scratch-resistant lenses. (please see note - I might mean reflection-free) OR just don't shower whilst wearing them.

- Buy spectacles with advanced hinge elastic technology.
- Just start drawing! (Even all over this book!)
- Find a safe environment with good friends or strangers to talk about your feelings. Good friends will understand.
- Be assertive
- Learn to be love.
- Get an individual artist's 'look', so people will remember you.
- Save money: don't bother getting your hair cut.
- Focus on a big project of your own.
- Make a book containing your own work.
- Dress smartly for your video marketing.
- Cultivate holes in clothes.
- Always stand right behind your toddler as they climb the stairs.
- Put yourself on that pedestal.
- Check out my 'How to Be a Successful Artist' free videos and social media pages.

Take care my pretties.

Your Notes and Sketches